FROM MY DIARY

PAYAL K.

Made with ♥ on the Notion Press Platform
www.notionpress.com

TO MY FAMILY

WHO HAVE ALWAYS BELIEVED ON BETTING OVER

MY DREAMS ..

Contents

Contents

Contents

Contents

Foreword

This book , "FROM MY DIARY " is basically a collection of some simple poetries which were written by an amateur . But , still some simple words were quite efficient over a long speech of complicated words . Books are our bestfriend , who could be our companion . Similiarly , writing is her solace , no matter what issue it is , a little session of venting up with words can be enough to clear that mind , which is even messier than a bird's nest .

And, when it comes to mess who don't know , how complicated situtation of this life is , while tangling in these threads of emotions just act as cherry on top . It doesn't matter if it is love , carrier or any other relationships , confusions are always here . As a reader , I don't know , what would be your thoughts , but , if you ask from me , I would definately say , this book wasn't going to be a regret . Even though , it can't clear those confusions you had but , it can definately help you to have a fine time while , going through it's pages in your leisure .

Even though , I have read these chapters many times from a reader view , afterall being an introvert , I could rarely approach someone but , still I have posted few poetries and gladly response wasn't that bad . My only friend have read a few of mine creations and have appreciated them but , I want to look forward for your reviews.

I'm writing this foreword from the feedbacks , I have got from my virtual family over the past few years of writing story , who always support me and eagerly looking forward for it's release .

Preface

Writing novels , expressing characters dilemma is quite efficient topic . Even though , it's not that hard but , giving exactly readers , what you want to express is really a hardwork with essence of smartness . Well ! my novels were still on e platform and it's a long way to their physical form . Despite from this , I have always try to keep them first hand , it's different , I ended up changing everytime , I try to revise . Fortunately , making them better than before .

Getting in mood of characters , what need me is a warm song and writing a poetry on the situtation of chapters . These collection also hold a quite well yield of my imaginations but , since it was my first time , I wouldn't dare to say they are best one , afterall way is long .

And , about idea of having this book , Actually that wasn't hard to guess , as tittle was already telling , "From my Diary ". I used to write poems in my diary , which have already got filled with poems over two hundred , afterall what could be better hideout than these verses of words .

So , I decided to publish it on online platform but , seriously who don't want to see their creation being alive , and like everyone , I was also trying to find ways but, without money , it's little difficult . Thankfully , I got notionpress , it saved a lot , even though typing , editing and cover designing came in my block , it was worth it . Afterall , getting some skills aren't bad .

Even though , these poem can be sad and happy , they meant for nothing but, a casual read , when you were on your bed , letting the cold breeze hiting your face through the window of your room . It's different if you can relate to it , it's just a coincidence , don't look for me for your life's leak .

Acknowledgements

This book can't be able to here without the help of notionpress so , I really want to thank them for creating this opportunity for me to have my first physical book. This self publishing have took many new skills out from me , whether it's being editor or cover designer of this book .

I am thankful to wattpad for being a platform for me in connecting me with my readers , allowing me to grow every day .

And , special thanks to my friend shaily for being as eager as I'm , to have this book in my hands . Apart from that , I want to thank my all lovely readers whose efforts have taken me @Bindasspayal here especially to @amham123 , @hatesyy , @vedikasharma , @inhedatta and all my precious .

I want to thank my parents for being blessings to me . Lastly , I want to be grateful to neha and manya for being an existence in my life , supporting me in every rough and toughs .

Thank you ! to all those people for being a motivator of mine and those who have given their efforts for making , ' From my DIARY " alive.

Prologue

A mini diary to be
trash can of my heart ,
Those poetries which are going to be
words of my lost love,
Those facade ,
I got of being in love
were nothing but ,
My teen's first crush...

1. An Eulogy For Hidden Grief

Weaving this web of
hopelessness,
I have got a broken mirror of
my carelessness,
It's not, I'm still stubborn to
accept those arrays of failures
have got my feets
even after the reluctance of infinity
to stop chasing
that unattainable dream,
It's not even that,
I'm shadowing my sorrows
blaming the shatterings
of those hidden verses
behind some unexisting stream,
It's just,
I have seen those arrays of mistakes,
to emit that light,
I want to chase without having any
Regret...

2. Too Dreamy

Smiling at the silly jokes
of mine ,
You think I don't know about
those looks of your eyes
which turns into glitters
just after a single attention of mine,
I know ,
I'm being rude
Breaking your heart ,
But , what can I do
when I know
what you want for us
is too dreamy to be true...

3. Lovers of yours

The day , I saw you on your knees
carrying warmness of that love
I always wanted to see ,
I knew , what I'm going to lose
knowing well those glitters
didn't meant for me ,
still , I took the chance
showing you
reality of my heart,
But , in the end you just laughed
thanking me warmily
for being a good friend helping you
in chasing
lovers of yours...

4. Her Knight

No matter
how much heartless
Today
I seems to your eyes,
I know
there is still an appeareance of mine
which was hidden well
behind
those thick walls of this heart of mine,
A stupid enough to call you .
Her knight..

5. Second choice

Being the gentleman
for whom
everyone love to fall for,
carrying the cutest smile
I was just waiting for your call ,
But , I didn't got
why even being first to catch your eyes,
I still ended up
being a second choice ...

6. Anymore

Why these nights still felt lonely
when you are at my side ,
Don't know things changed or us ,
But, regret is only that
it doesn't matter me
anymore...

7. Vibe Check

Reading a rom -com
in these dim lights ,
suddenly ,
I got a vibe check with second lead
who ended up
being main lead's
second choice...

8. Your Realm

My mind travels
in world of fantasy with you ,
But , if I keep my thoughts aside
from these weird hypothesis of mine ,
Then ,
I want to see ,
if I exist in your world of dreams or
I'm just an unimportant stuff,
you are having in
your realm...

9. A Goodbye

Whenever I was in problem
I have always got
these charming view of yours,
But ,the question is
now when I know why you are the one
whom I meet
everytime I had a foul time,
you bid me a goodbye
saying you had no right,
to stay
at my side...

10. Love To Hate

Every soap opera story
starts from hate
and end to love
Hope , mine life could be a soap opera
Atleast ,
I have got love in the end
rather than being ,
A love to hate thing...

11. Non living Being

Praising about smiles
I carry over my lips,
you expect me to accept
you confession ,
even knowing these smiles
were just facade over,
my non living being...

12. Aren't ?

Aren't you are too proud of being
reason for my red cheeks ,
Aren't you are too obvious
about the day we will never meet,
Don't you know
you are the only peace
which can make me tease,
still you dare to left me
on those steps
from where we can never
meet...

13. Unnoticeable

First ray of sun
that fall on me
The wind
which makes my hair
to flow on or in ,
Hope , you could be same ,
like the sun and wind ,
selfless yet unnoticeable ,
unknown to my dreams...

14. Keys

The boy
whom I saw on his knees
why ?
become the one
who want my
keys...

15. Dreaming

With these slow winds
I'm waiting for your love rains
to fall over my realm ,
Maybe , I'm a hate daydreamer
but, what's wrong in dreaming
when it's you ,
who is coming allover again
in my sleeps...

16. Moonlight

You are the warmness
that my heart wants to have
at every cold nights,
you are the solace
for which I yearn
at every foul time ,
you are the happiness
I always want at my side ,
Hope , this you could you ,
who is standing with rose for me ,
in this broad moonlight...

17. Standing Behind

Picking the most bloomed rose
from these bouque of redness,
why will your beautiful sight
will even land
on that dried rose in side,
which have lost it's chance
just because of
standing behind...

18. Get a Handsome

They say ,
A beauty can turn
A beast into human ,
If that's what that fairy tale of legends say ,
could I get a handsome
to intiate a saga of this witch
who will become an angel
without having any devil ,
standing behind
for her retreat...

19. Someone else Smile

In those late nights,
you don't know
how many times I have cried,
But, the question is
why I'm telling you ,
it isn't that
I don't know in those nights
you are busy in being
someone else smile...

20. Demise

Reading novels
don't know when my eyes paused at a poetry line,
I'm not worried
about my life's leak ,
It's just , I'm scared
why I'm hating character of you ,
when in real life
I'm waiting for you ,
even after my heart's
demise...

21. Everytime

Under the dark night sky
siting beside this cold water lake ,
sorrounded by these sweet yellow light of fireflies
I'm waiting for your arrival
with a lonely smile ,
Tell me ,
if you really gonna to come or not,
cause ,
I can't pretend to be happy forever
when it's you,
who is hurting me
everytime...

22. Beautiful Lie

There was a time
I used to laugh
like a flower which is up to rise ,
Then , came a beautiful lie !
As gorgeous as those snow flakes
As fresh like morning sun rays
that beautiful made me smile ,
uncaring about the bad days ,
I always try to hide.
That lie seemed to be
most beautiful happenings of my life,
But , soon the reality check came from nowhere
being the worst strom ,
breaking every flowery bubble of mine.
I got to know
what was true
maybe , not what I imagined
to be true ,
I got a mirror of reality ,
But , it wasn't as gorgeous as
those lie of yours,
Maybe , because it showed me the feeling

what people call , broke !
Those love we made
those blushes we had
those smiles we share
were nevers in your eyes to care.
But , now no lie is lie to me
I knew about my reality ,
where I was nothing in your sight ,
you have left adding nothing but ,
a big chapter in this memory bin of mine,
being nothing but,
a beautiful lie to forgive but ,
impossible to forget even after
my demise...

23. Stuck

Ways you had for me
Aim you got for me,
Why I think is meaning less now ,
Tell me ,
is it me or you
who is at fault
when the one
who left stuck
is me...

24. Unexpressed Love

Desires are too heavy for my heart
let alone the lust ,
So , you tall beast ,
if you can hear these voices of my heart ,
I guess we both were stuck
in this ocean of society
on the small boat of our
unexpressed love...

25. City of Love

Meeting secretly
on the backside of my house,
who says there is nothing
like a city of love
Come on ! I can debate on that ,
Afterall , I have seen and felt every imaginations
of that city of love
Just standing at my back door,
gazing the same moon ,
he used to admire
from siting beside my door...

26. Dreams

Crying for attention ,
Rhyming in these fields,
I'm waiting
for a reality check
for some impractical
dreams...

27. Insecure

Maybe these words of love
will never reach you ,
Maybe these emotions of my eyes
will never meant to you,
But , what can I do about myself
Afterall , it was never may from my side ,
But , away from those dust of past,
now you have changed
But , don't know why ,
I was too insecure
about this togetherness with you
for lifetime...

28. Stay Here

Drenching in rain
remebering those promises
which are broken now,
you have left
But , I was thinking about the time we had ,
Getting nothing
expect that ring in my hand
I got this meant to be here
Afterall , that proud figure never meant
to stay here...

29. First Crush

Rhyming to music late night,
I was remembering
old days with my closed eyes,
Like a synapse
everything came in front of my eyes
Smiling at those memories ,
I laughed at my first crush choice ,
sharing his food
in a lunch time...

30. Ignored Star

Admiring stars ,
I don't even got
when they turned into
a meteor shower ,
making night beautiful
with their unrecognizable sacrifice ,
Hope , you could able recognize
that ignored star you had
before it turns into ashes
crying for a single glance from
your eyes...

31. Another Poem

Standing in blue cinderella gown
I'm waiting for you in this ball night,
seeing you from crowds
admiring you from far ,
I'm hell nervous from that butterfly crowd,
so , tell me you tormentor of mine
Aren't you going to get me
after this fall ,
If yes , then just leave this teasing session tonight
and , start this saga of love ,
inviting me for a dance on our song
initiating rhyme
of another poem...

32. Hundred Miles

Brightening my night
with your presence,
I'm not disappointed
with this ignoreance of yours
coming after these years of separation ,
Afterall , it's not ,
I'm here to listen
how your heart shutters
at my every sight .
even after hating me for years
from those
hundred miles...

33. Nerd

Gazing the night sky
with my dull eyes,
hiding my love
behind those thick glasses of mine ,
yeah ! I'm the same nerd
waiting for my prince
to notice me between hundred stars while ,
admiring them under the
moonlight...

34. My Fantasy

Like the music of cricket
at night ,
you are the angel
who came in my dream every night ,
I don't know
if I'm suffering from any disease
or it's just my fantasy that
I'm craving for
your sight...

35. Turn off the fire

Don't be always confident
to know me ,
Sometimes ,
even water can't able to
turn off the
fire...

36. Soulmate

Soulmate is like
the another page of notebook
Different yet inseparable...

37. Let me forget you

Everytime,
you forget me ,
But , this time
let me forget you...

38. Peace

Telling lies to make me
to leave you ,
Aren't you taking me as
same egoistic being you first meet,
I don't know
what words can change your mind ,
But, see in my eyes
I'm sure you can find that same peace
you have seen once in
these eyes...

39. Forever Mine

I wanted
moon to be mine ,
But , I forgot
it only appears in the night ,
While , I wanted it to be
forever mine...

40. A Fantasy

Hope ,
tales exist in some reality
Cause ,
I don't want
what I dreamt ,
just end up being
a fantasy...

41. The way I hadn't taken

The way I got
hope , I had taken that
Atleast ,
I wouldn't be regreting
about the way ,
I hadn't taken...

42. Spoke up

A lame excuse
to broke up with me ,
Aren't you was the same boy
who wanted
to spoke up with
me...

43. Without any remorse

Lies you said,
promises you broke
tears I had
for those facade you gave
under those smiles cover of yours,
I don't have much wish for compensation ,
it's just
I wanted to be that warrior
to feel that glory
you felt while killing this heart of mine
without any remorse..

44. Dark Clouds

Dark clouds
taking the sky ,
while , rain standing at my door ,
Do you really think
I can wait,
when it's you
who is moving
out of my approach...

45. Congratulations

Red rose in your hand
was telling me enough
About the new happiness you had
congratulations for the addition
you had ,
And , sorry for the subtraction
you gonna to
have...

46. Letters of past

Tearing these letter's of our past
I don't even got
when I got sorrounded by
these trashes ,
wonder that only comes to my mind
when I turned this fool
that those conspiracies of yours became
unnoticed to

my eyes...

47. Toy

Waiting for you
in the vast starlight,
Tired of pretending
to love this night ,
Come on !
How much games you want to play
when it's me,
who is turning a toy
with each passing time...

48. My sight

Reciting those letters once
you have wrote for me ,
Rembering those emotions
which have passed once within me ,
My eyes have turned empty
craving for your sight ,
Are you really not going to come
saying that love
have left only in
my sight...

49. A Fool

Seeing these dandelions
remembering the myth,
I'm trying to blow it's seeds
in a single breath,
But , what can this flower even do ,
when it's you
who is hell bent in
making me
a fool...

50. Devil and Angel

Running away from devil,
Still ending with it's beast,
Don't tell me,
you still don't get what we are
A devil and an angel
meant to fall,
always off the
deal...

51. Strangers

Call me fake
when I say about the timepause
I have at every sight of yours,
Locking my eyes with gaze of yours
I pass without a single word
running out from throat,
Truely , it would be fake
if I call those feelings love
that I felt at every mention of you
in those past lonely years,
Afterall who were
nothing but, strangers
who were
never known...

52. Unrelatble Stuff

Humming music
in this late night,
Feeling it's lyrics
revealing my life,
Smiling at the irony,
I can even relate
to an unknown song in a first time,
And, you were accusing me
for being the most unrelatble stuff
in your sight...

53. His Side

Having bitter wine
down my throat ,
watching your moves
from the top floor ,
Maybe , I'm a cold hearted stalker
from other eyes,
But , you know
what this cold hearted want ?
a warmness emiting from your brows
to his side...

54. Plees

Love is the only risk
I had taken ,
Even when I knew
I'm going to stay alone
at the end ,
seeing you choosing someone else
ignoring my every
plees...

55. Fallen Angel

I may be a fallen angel
But , believe me
My burned wings can
even turn sky
into ashes,
So , think before
messing with this angel
cause even if you are king of hell,
I'm owning
a hell in heaven...

56. Yours

My mind shadows
still heart find a ray ,
My feets stops
still hands want to stay,
I don't know rhyming as much
your eyes do,
But , I can say ,
I had done enough poetry
after crashing
into this way of
yours...

57. First Sight

Being the princess
you only know to hold
your pillow tight
to stop chasing dinosaur
in your dreams at night,
How can you even think
to travel in my world of darkness
just carrying light of your soul
in immaturity of chasing
that love of
first sight...

Downtime

Being the princess

surely I hold my pillow tight

avoiding dinosaur crawling

into my bed at night ,

But , who told you

I will need to care about

darkness or a big dinosaur

when you are the brightest star of my sky

accompanying me at every

downtime...

58. Lady of Palace

Oh ! you lady of palace
you want to have me
at your side,
Then , tell me
how that beauty
can walk over thorns ,
who was even cared at a single tear
falling from
her beautiful doe eyes...

Lifetime

Might be ,

I'm even cared at a single tear

falling from my eyes ,

But , who told you

I can't walk on thorns

carrying smile of happiness

when it' you,

who is walking with me,

holding my hands for

lifetime...

59. Golden Realm

Having immaturity
you are even confused
about the dresses
you want to wear tonight ,
Then , tell me how can
you are sure
about this man with nothing
whom you want at
your every up and down
rise for you in that
golden realm which will never
accept him...

Sparks

Truly I'm confused

about the dresses

I want to wear everytime,

But , these are not because I'm immature,

it's just,

I want to see sparks

in those man's eyes

who was carrying nothing but ,

my heart at his side...

60. Innocence

Being a bad man
you maybe worst in people eyes,
But , to me
you are nothing but ,
a man who wanted to live
but, got death lords to kill
that heart of his
which used to beat an innocence
to live...

61. Everytime

Loving that brightest star
from down ,
how I forgot
why it even needed to see down
when it's moon is standing
just next to him
Everytime...

Vast sky

Yeah ! being near the moon

will never needed me to see down ,

But , what can I do

I just wanted to be

a single star in that vast sky of yours

which would only

mine...

62. Sadistic

My tears have dried
crying buckets for you,
And you dare to call me
a betrayer,
after moving on from
a sadistic
like you...

63. Deepest Valleys

64. What I meant ?

Calling you mine
in end of every convo
we hit ,
still you don't got
what I meant..

65. Cute

Truly a stupid one
you were,
Afterall ,
how a smart person can't get
it's my way of calling you
cute...

66. Perfect

You used to call me stupid
for always thinking me
through my heart,
Sorry ! I can't even blame god to
send an imperfect in perfect world of yours,
Maybe , I'm just too selfish for that ,
But , I can give you your happiness
after giving this last letter
of that stupid one,
taking that one away
from that perfect world of
yours...

Imperfectness

After this departure of yours

I got ,

you were making my life

perfect

while , carrying my imperfectness with

yours...

67. Meet

Chasing those mistakes
my teenself did ,
Yeah ! I'm still waiting for you
on the steps
from where you said
we will never

meet...

68. Day one

I'm not sad
seeing those sparkles in your eyes
for someone else,
it's just , I'm disappointed
you can't hear crumbling of
your friend's heart
whom you are too proud to know
from the day one
you meet...

69. Really!

Really !
I'm the princess of your world ,
Then tell me ,
why I'm standing in these plain clothes
having nothing but , my torn heart
beating lightly inside
my chest bone...

70. Cupid in Love

Accepting the fact
slow steps can be cute in a love story ,
I don't know
when I made my fun reaching your love
Being a cupid
in this lovestory of
yours...

71. Benefactor

Tearing this bindation of limits
I have ran to world of yours ,
Forgetting every norms of my world
I have come to this world of yours,
so, just wait a little more for us
my tormenter,
cause your princess
is just few steps away
to be your
benefactor...

72. Stone Heart

73. Facade of love

What a great buisnessman
you are,
Afterall
who will knew to trade
love for the revenge,
you have hidden over the
facade of love...

74. Crazy Bird

Standing alone
on the steps,
from where
we can never meet,
yeah! I'm a crazy bird
who still wants to stay in cage
after getting
free...

75. Hide and Seek

Colouring this world of mine
with this redness of your love,
you have smeared my realm
with chaoticness of
this hide and seek
love...

76. Hidden Feels

Coming together
till the end of this shaky road,
we waved a goodbye
with hidden glitters and a fake smile
shining on our face ,
Can't for a second
just we can keep our facade aside,
to give a chance to those feels
who have always hidden
inside those
unknown heart's
doors...

77. Twirl

Standing in field
of dandelion,
I'm loving the way
they sway with the breeze ,
unaware from the fact
these winds were making them
to lose their existence
with every twirl...

78. Lover Boy

Wandering in these streets
of yours,
My eyes were moving up to see
a smily face
from terrace of yours,
still you tell me it's me being a pervert
not a lover boy of yours,
who want nothing but
to get a peek of his moon ,
indifferent from the clouds
who have blocked
his view...

79. Off the Shore

80. Past Dreams

Reciting those letters
you have sent
in fooling days of your teens,
a smile lingered my lips
thinking about how smart
that boy have became
forgetting
his past dreams...

81. Dark Romance

Trying to betray me
with those pretty eyes of yours ,
Do you really think me
as some naive lead of dark romance,
to forget every sins of yours
just with a sorry
left from cunning mouth of
yours...

82. Bad Boy

Being the bad boy
I was habitatuted for the curses
coming in my way,
But , why being the good girl
you are coming in
bad boy's ways...

83. Good Girl

Carrying the
good girl's card
I was living well
Then, why you came
with bad boy identity of yours
destroying every facade
I had...

84. Farewell's Bid

Recalling our first dance at
fresher's meet,
I'm gazing at your smily face
which was busy with her partner,
doing last dance in
farewell's bid...

85. Our Love

Loving that cuteness
of your face
when anger rushes out from your veins,
I didn't even got
when our relation also got
tainted by this cuteness of yours ,
and I stood unaffected
seeing fall of that castle we made
in blooming phase of
our love...

86. Heartless

Those defeats never gave me
that much sorrows
as much your lies gave me,
The hurt you planned for me
is already completed
Then, tell me
why being my heartless
is reason for those empty eyes of
yours...

87. Among Rest

Admiring the best
I didn't even got
those gazes
in which I turned
among rest...

88. Someone else

Listening the lovely song
I'm imagining our lovely dance on it,
swaying in your arms
with the lusturious beats,
But , wait !
Doesn't those arms meant for
someone else...

89. My Sight

Lying above my pillow
I was trying to imagine my hero
with close eyes ,
But , I never knew
it was my close eyes
which was restricting your view
to my sight...

90. Accidental Meet

Starting a saga
we meet as a stranger
always falling off the deal,
still destiny always throwed us together
in the same bin ,
And , when we know , what we are
you are okay in ending all this
just saying we were friends
who became close after
an accidental meet...

91. Cinderella

Tales tells,
cinderella ran away
her prince charming found her,
Then ,
why in my case ?
when I ran
my prince got another princess...

92. Bleed

After breaking my heart
you are back,
wanting another chance
to heal me,
Then , try to get those pieces
you shattered,
Let me even see
if those bleeds were only meant for me,
or really !
these broken pieces are
indifferent to everyone
making them bleed...

93. Doesn't me

Listening these chaoes of
weeding bells,
it isn't ,
standing in this dark corner
I'm sulking over my loss,
Infact , it's this glory of
your happiness
which was crumbling my heart
telling about the heartbeats
residing in your heart
doesn't belong to me
anymore...

94. Too Bloody

Shattering those glasses
in my hand,
I was seeing those red fountain flowing down
through my palms,
well! it's not ,
I have a troubling desire in my heart,
It's just the memories you left
were too bloody
to even remorse without a
single shot of this dreamy alcholic liquid
moving down my throat...

95. Still in me

My eyes on her but,
hers were waiting for
someone else,
she is gone but , question is
when she was with me ?
Aren't we were enemies
or there was always something else ,
Whatever the thing was
irony is her every tear kills me and her every smile
are still in me ...

96. Artifact

You were the most preserved artifact
that I had in my collection,
Then ,
what happened you became
unattainable to even enter my sight
forgetting everey special meeting
I used to hide...

97. Left one

One sided love ,
selfless
Two sided love ,
fortunate
Hate to love,
destiny
But , incomplete love is true love,
They said me ,
when they left
Then , why I'm seeing them,
saying the same
words to that one ,
who is going to be another
left one...

98. Hundred Smiles

Standing in this moonlight
when everyone is busy in gazing night
filled with star sight .
I'm admiring your gazes
trying to find me
between hundred smiles...

99. Dust of craziness

What is there to even
remember
when you had left nothing to
forget ,
But , still let me ask you
if your feets have got their way to me
forgetting there was even a time
when we were us ,
Is really , I was a fool to destroy my everything
under the dust of craziness,
I misinterpreted to call
Love...

100. Beauty

Reading those letters
you left to tell tale of
your love,
I'm trying to escape from the fact
I was the beauty
who rejected the blessing of
your love...

101. I commit!

Falling for you was never in list
still I did,
Intentionally or Unintentionally
I did,
Call me fool or lover boy of yours,
In the end
it's crime of love
what I commit...

I think , it would be bulky , if I add them anymore in it .

Thank you , for looking for my first physical and overall fourth book in my creation .

If you want to read more and my old books , you can come on wattpad , where I live as @Bindasspayal . You can talk and share your views with me , and cherry on the top get access to my free books , as originally I'm more into writing novels in the genre of romantic thriller .

Hope , you have loved this little collection of mine , while , having a nice time . Once again thankyou ! I would be waiting for your feedbacks and , don't forget to tell me your favorite one of these all .